Summary

of

The Tea Girl of Hummingbird Lane
Lisa See

Conversation Starters

By BookHabits

Tips for Using BookHabits Conversation Starters:

EVERY GOOD BOOK CONTAINS A WORLD FAR DEEPER THAN the surface of its pages. The characters and their world come alive through the words on the pages, yet the characters and its world still live on. Questions herein are designed to bring us beneath the surface of the page and invite us into the world that lives on. These questions can be used to:

- Foster a deeper understanding of the book
- Promote an atmosphere of discussion for groups
- Assist in the study of the book, either individually or corporately
- Explore unseen realms of the book as never seen before

About Us:

THROUGH YEARS OF EXPERIENCE AND FIELD EXPERTISE, from newspaper featured book clubs to local library chapters, *BookHabits* can bring your book discussion to life. Host your book party as we discuss some of today's most widely read books.

Table of Contents

Introducing *The Tea Girl of Hummingbird Lane*

*T*HE TEA GIRL OF HUMMINGBIRD LANE IS THE 12TH AND latest of Lisa See's novels which are known for their Chinese characters, historical setting in China, and highlighting women's complex relationships with each other. See's first book, *On Gold Mountain: The One Hundred Year Odyssey of my Chinese-American Family* tells the story of See's great-grandfather who became the godfather of Chinatown in Los Angeles and the patriarch of See's large family. This national bestseller was followed by three mystery novels, also revolving around Chinese lives, earned critics' respect. These were further followed by See's bestseller historical novels which focused on women and their strong bonds, while illuminating

China's historical past and the people who lived during those times.

She continues her storytelling prowess in her newest novel, using the same outstanding research skills, to interweave contemporary themes of international adoption, the ethnic culture of the Akha in China, global tea trade, and the strong bonds between mothers and daughters. The result is what Goodreads review calls "thrilling" and "powerful", and according to Booklist, "an extraordinary homage to unconditional love."

Li-yan is one of the few educated girls in her tribe who can deal with businessmen who want to bring Pu'er, the tea leaves her people have been cultivating for many generations, to the global market. She learns new things about tea business that her people have very little knowledge of. This opens new paths for her.

Growing up with her Akha family, she learns how to grow and gather tea leaves even as she learns her role as a girl in the tribe-- one who must be subordinate to the decisions of the men. As she becomes aware of the traditional beliefs and ritual of her people, she slowly sees things she does not approve of. Her mother, the tribe's midwife, follows rules about eliminating babies whom the tribal elders call human rejects, including twins and babies born out of wedlock. She criticizes rules like these, but she is just a girl, and does not have a voice that will be listened to. Not even when she objects to her parents' mandate that she cannot be with the man she loves. According to their birth signs, she and San-pa are not going to be a happy couple. She gets pregnant anyway and the baby, born out of wedlock, would not have survived if Li-yan's mother, the midwife, did not defy tribal rules. Li-yan brings her baby to an orphanage in the city who eventually gets adopted by an American couple. Li-yan and San-pa reunite and she goes back to the orphanage to get her baby back. She finds herself too late-- the American couple brought the baby with them to the US. Li-yan spends many years of her life trying to connect to her lost baby. Tea business provides Li-yan the opportunity to leave for the city, and eventually for the US where she hopes to reunite with her daughter.

See's well-researched account of the Akha and their culture reveal many interesting, even shocking things about the tribe, which led a New York Times reviewer to call it "dystopic." Along with their tea making tradition, their culture's unique ways are woven into the story stirring the curiosity of readers about the lives of ethnic minorities in China. The tea motif is introduced to readers at the start of the novel, accompanies Li-yan through her difficulties, and is a key element that will finally connect Li-yan and her daughter. Further adding to the rich narrative is See's account of the complexities of global tea trade, one that highlights China's role in international trade and provides insight to globalization. Likewise, the international adoption process is given attention by See's superb research into the work and drama that goes with it make the novel even more engaging.

See tells the story of Li-yan's daughter, Haley, through emails, doctors' notes, and Haley's writing homework. Through these notes, readers learn of the difficult, complex feelings Haley has for her adoptive and birth parents. See's use of this device introduces Haley in a distant way, without a voice of her own, unlike Li-yan whose narrative voice allows readers to know her closely.

See dedicated the novel to her mother, Carolyn See, who died in 2016. Her mother was a bestseller author herself who taught See her storytelling skills. The novel's focus on the undying bonds between mothers and daughters, by birth or adoption, is a fitting homage to her mother who inspired See to write her

beautiful stories.

Introducing the Author

L ISA SEE IS BEST KNOWN FOR HER BESTSELLER HISTORICAL fiction novels set in China. Her latest and 12th book, *The Tea Girl of Hummingbird Lane* published in March 2017 is written along the same vein, following her multiple New York Times bestselling titles. These novels have been lauded for genuine and powerfully evoked stories of Chinese characters and the times they lived in. See is also cited for her high-level research on her subjects which included controversial Chinese cultural practices like foot binding, and a thousand-year old secret writing practice by women.

Before her historical fiction became popular she wrote mystery novels with Chinese-related themes and were critically acclaimed. *Flower Net*, her first novel published in 1997, was a national bestseller, a NY Times Notable Book, and was in the Best Books List of the Los Angeles Times. Her two other mystery-thrillers, *The Interior* (2000) and *Dragon Bones* (2003) had critics comparing See to Upton Sinclair, Dashiell Hammet, and Sir Arthur Conan Doyle. Her first book *"On Gold Mountain,"* published in 1995, tackled the history of Chinese migration to California and her family's experience. The book tells the story her great-great-grandfather who first arrived in the US to help build the transcontinental railroad. This paved the way for her great-grandfather to establish himself as the godfather and patriarch of Chinatown in Los Angeles.

Ms. See is one-eighth Chinese and has drawn much inspiration from the stories of her large Chinese-American family in Los Angeles. Straddling both American and Chinese cultures, See wants her readers to understand that despite cultural differences, all people have the same life experiences and share the same emotions like love, jealousy, greed, hate. A recurrent theme in her books is women's relationships. Different kinds of relationships among women, all uniquely female, are explored in her novels. She believes that not enough stories about women in history have been told, and telling those stories that have been particularly forgotten or lost is an important task for her. It is because history is also composed of women, children and the elderly, and not just of men.

Her identity as part-Chinese and part-American has given her a point of view which helped her as a writer. She is considered an outsider among the Chinese communities or in China because of her skin and red hair, and does not feel she truly belongs to the white community either. According to her, being an outsider makes her a better writer.

See claims that it was her mother Carolyn See, herself a bestseller writer, who influenced her to write. In a recorded dialogue between mother and daughter, See told her mother that she learned her storytelling skills from Carolyn. Other major influences were Bob Dylan who she considers a genius, and Wallace Stegner.

See was active as the West Coast correspondent for Publishers Weekly for over a decade. Apart from writing and researching for her novels, See had time to write for Los Angeles Opera, was a guest curator at the Autry Museum of Western, likewise curating the Family Discovery Gallery which featured her bi-racial childhood in the perspective of her father's boyhood living in Los Angeles during the 30's.

Discussion Questions

"Get Ready to Enter a New World"

Tip: Begin with questions dealing with broader issues to ensure ample time for quality discussions. Read through all discussion questions before engaging.

~ ~ ~

question 1

Author Lisa See is known for her historical fiction including the New York Times bestsellers *Snow Flower and the Secret Fan* and *Peony in Love,* both of which are set in China. Why do you think her novels are appealing to so many readers? Does the mention of China and Chinese culture stir your interest in reading the book?

~ ~ ~

~ ~ ~

question 2

The main character of the story, Li-Yan, belongs to the ethnic
minority, the Akha, in China. Do you think author Lisa See's
portrayal of the Akha is authentic? What was required of her as
author to do a genuine portrayal of the ethnic tribe? Would the
novel have been interesting if the setting did not involve an
ethnic culture?

~ ~ ~

~~~

question 3

At the beginning of the novel, Li-yan, the protagonist, quotes her mother saying "No coincidence, no story." Why do you think the author opens the first chapter with these words? Do coincidences play a significant part in the novel? What are the most important coincidences and how crucial are they in the novel's plot?

~~~

~ ~ ~

question 4

The Akha's age-old tradition of growing tea is a key part of the novel. How is the tea theme woven in the novel's plot? Would you say the novel would have been just as interesting if the author did not devote time to narrate the particularities of tea culture?

~ ~ ~

question 5

Li-yan recounts the many beliefs and practices of her tribe including dream interpretation and the cleansing ritual to rectify a misdeed such as stealing. Do you think the future generations of Akha will continue to keep these beliefs and practices along with the influences from outsiders/ tea businessmen?

~~~

question 6

The Akha people believe that children born out of wedlock and twins are considered human rejects and should not be allowed to live. The midwife-- and mother of Li-yan-- ensures that the unwanted babies don't survive. Why do you think the Akha came to practice this? Does survival of the tribe in its early years have something to do with this?

~~~

~~~

question 7

Li-yan gave birth to a child out of wedlock and gave the baby to an orphanage instead of following the tribe's rules against human rejects. Do you think it was an easy decision for her? Can you imagine how it is for a girl like her to defy the whole tribe?

~~~

~ ~ ~

question 8

As one of the few educated girls in her tribe Li-yan dealt with businessmen who wanted to market their tea. Would you say education among ethnic people is a good thing? Are there any negative aspects to this?

~ ~ ~

~~~

question 9

Li-yan's daughter Haley is introduced in the novel through letters, psychotherapist's notes, and written homework assignments. Were you able to get a good grasp of Haley's character and life circumstances through these devices? Is the use of written documents a good way to narrate that part of the novel?

~~~

~~~

question 10

Li-yan's mother A-ma defied tribal rules against babies out of wedlock and allowed Li-yan's baby to live. How would you relate her mother's courage to Li-yan's yearning and fervent search for her lost daughter? Was the novel successful in portraying strong connection between mothers and daughters?

~~~

~ ~ ~

question 11

A chapter of the novel shows how Chinese-American adoptees have difficult feelings about their birth and adoptive families. Were you able to understand the anger they felt? Would you feel the same if you were in their shoes?

~ ~ ~

~ ~ ~

question 12

The women in Li-yan's village hold subordinate position to the men. Li-yan's mother however has the tribe's respect for being the midwife. How important is her role? Do you think she has more power than what the men in her tribe acknowledge?

~ ~ ~

~~~

question 13

The global tea business enabled Li-yan to leave her village and pursue her dream to see the daughter she gave up for adoption. Do you think global business enables women like Li-yan to gain independence and a certain amount of empowerment? Do you see any negative effects?

~~~

question 14

For many years, Li-yan and her daughter Haley have been each thinking of the other although they have never met. When mother and daughter finally meet, how do you think each will relate to the other? Do you think Haley will be able to appreciate her ethnic roots?

~~~

question 15

The relationship of Li-Yan and San-pa was frowned upon by their families because their birth animals are incompatible. They proceeded to have a relationship anyway but it ends tragically. Do you think they would have been a happy couple if their families did not give too much weight on their beliefs? Why or why not?

~~~

~~~

question 16

Though still about Chinese culture, *The Tea Girl of Hummingbird Lane* is different from Lisa See's other books because it tackles a Chinese ethnic minority tribe, the Akha, instead of the Chinese majority, the Han. Do you think readers will just be just as interested? Why? Why not?

~~~

~~~

question 17

The Washington Times review says the novel's story is "shaped by globalization." Do you agree with this opinion? In what ways is the story shaped by globalization?

~~~

~~~

question 18

The New York Times Book Review says the novel is set in a
"superstitious and dystopian world". The author Lisa See is also
known for doing thorough research on her subjects, the Akha
tribe in this case. Do you agree with the description of dystopian?
What does this imply about the Akha tribe?

~~~

~~~

question 19

Goodreads describes the novel as "thrilling" and "powerful". Did you go through the same emotional journey when you read the novel? Why or why not?

~~~

~~~

question 20

Booklist reviewer praises the novel as a "complex narrative" but thinks that readers may consider the ending unbelievable. Do you agree with this evaluation? Why? Why not?

~~~

~~~

question 21

The Tea Girl of Hummingbird Lane is dedicated to Lisa See's mother, Carolyn See, who died in July 2016. Carolyn was professor emerita of English at the University of California, Los Angeles and authored ten books. Do you think Lisa would have been as successful without her mother's influence on her as a writer?

~~~

question 22

Though highly influenced by her mother, See admits that it was her paternal grandmother who had the greatest influence on her because she was adventurous and unconventional. Would have it been possible for See to write her interesting and strong women characters without her grandmother's impact on her life?

~~~

question 23

See is bi-racial and feels like an outsider in both the Chinese and white communities. This has been an advantage for her as writer because it makes her more aware and more sensitive to racial differences. Do you think she is a better writer because of her of being an outsider?

~~~

~~~

question 24

See likes to tell stories of women that would have otherwise been lost, forgotten or covered up, as a result of history's focus on men. Why do you think it is important for her to tell these kinds of stories? Are the stories of Li-yan, A-ma, and Haley worth telling?

~~~

~~~

question 25

See's extensive research is central to her books. This not only meant poring over old documents in libraries but also going to far-flung villages in China and spending time with the tribal people. Would the novel have been equally interesting if there had been less attention to research?

~~~

~~~

question 26

Li-yan's mother decided to let Li-yan bring the baby to an orphanage instead of ending the baby's life which was the tribal rule. If Li-yan's mother decided instead to keep the baby with them and defy tribal tradition, what do you think would have happened? Do you think the women would rally behind her?

~~~

~~~

question 27

The novel's ending points toward the eventual reunion of Li-Yan and and her daughter Haley. If you were Haley, how would you accommodate Li-Yan into your life? Upon knowing of your Akha origins and culture, how will you react to your mother's tribal beliefs and traditions?

~~~

~~~

question 28

San-pa, Haley's father, eventually dies in the story leaving Li-Yan to solely search for their daughter. If he survived and reunited with his daughter, do you think it would have been a better ending or story? Why? Why not?

~~~

~~~

question 29

Author Lisa See did a lot of research about the Akha in order to write the novel, going to their far-flung villages and watching them do their tea farming. If she based her story of an ethnic tribe purely on imagination, how do you think the novel would have come out? Would it have been as interesting and rich in details?

~~~

~~~

question 30

The author implied that the novel will end in a reunion of mother and daughter. If the reunion does not happen, will the story be just as captivating? Why? Why not?

~~~

~~~

question 31

For her research, See visited Mengsung, a well-known pu'er producing area within Xishuangbanna Prefecture; the Nannuo Mountain; and Yiwu of the famous Ancient Tea Horse Route. She was guided by Linda Louie, owner of Bana Tea Company which sells Pu'er tea in the US.

~~~

~~~

question 32

Lisa See types her books on her laptop with only three fingers.

~~~

~ ~ ~

question 33

One of See's novels, Snow Flower and the Secret Fan was made into a feature film produced by Fox Searchlight.

~ ~ ~

~ ~ ~

question 34

See's great-grandfather, godfather of Los Angeles Chinatown, had three Chinese wives and one white, all at the same time.

~ ~ ~

~ ~ ~

question 35

See used the pen name Monica Highlight when she co-wrote
books with her mother and their friend John Espey.

~ ~ ~

~~~

question 36

While looking into the tea production process, See was surprised to see that the ancient tea trees "barely overgrow a human," instead of looming large as she expected.

~~~

question 37

However, she says the King of the Ancient Tea Trees is 14.7 meters high, is over 800 years old, and is a famous tourist attraction.

~~~

question 38

Her favorite teacher, apart from her mother, was Mrs. Bruinslot, her fifth grade teacher who loved history and made it come alive.

~~~

Quiz Questions

"Ready to Announce the Winners?"

Tip: Create a leaderboard and track scores to see who gets the most correct answers. Winners required. Prizes optional.

~ ~ ~

quiz question 1

True or False: All of Lisa See's historical fiction are set in Korea.

~ ~ ~

~~~

quiz question 2

True or False: The novel features characters inspired by the Chinese ethnic majority, the Han.

~~~

~ ~ ~

quiz question 3

The novel opens with Li-yan quoting her mother saying
_____.

~ ~ ~

quiz question 4

True or False: The Akha tradition of growing tea is a key theme in the novel.

~~~

quiz question 5

True or False: Dream interpretation is an important belief of the Akha.

~~~

~~~

quiz question 6

True or False: Babies born out of wedlock are welcomed by the Akha tribe.

~~~

~~~

quiz question 7

True or False: At the end of the novel, Li-yan is reunited with her daughter Ming.

~~~

~~~

quiz question 8

True or False: The novel was dedicated to Carolyn See, Lisa's mother.

~~~

quiz question 9

True or False: See's great-grandfather had the greatest influence on her.

~~~

quiz question 10

True or False: Being bi-racial and feeling like an outsider did not help See to become a good writer.

~~~

~~~

quiz question 11

True or False: It is important for See to write about men whose stories have been lost or forgotten.

~~~

~ ~ ~

quiz question 12

True or False: See traveled to China to research on her novel.

~ ~ ~

Quiz Answers

1. False
2. False
3. No coincidence, no story
4. True
5. True
6. False
7. False
8. True
9. False
10. False
11. False
12. True

Ways to Continue Your Reading

EVERY month, our team runs through a wide selection of books to pick the best titles for readers and reading groups, and promotes these titles to our thousands of readers – sometimes with free downloads, sale dates, and additional brochures.

Want to register yourself or a book group? It's free and takes 1-click.

Register here.

On the Next Page...

Please write us your reviews! Any length would be fine but we'd appreciate hearing you more! We'd be SO grateful.

Till next time,

BookHabits

"Loving Books is Actually a Habit"

Made in the USA
Lexington, KY
01 August 2019